Orca Origins

Nikki Tate & Dani Tate-Stratton

CHRISTMAS

From Solstice to Santa

ORCA BOOK PUBLISHERS

Library and Archives Canada Cataloguing in Publication

Tate, Nikki, 1962–, author
Christmas: from solstice to Santa / Nikki Tate & Dani Tate-Stratton.
(Orca origins)

Includes bibliographical references and index.

Issued in print and electronic formats.
ISBN 978-1-4598-1355-7 (hardcover).—ISBN 978-1-4598-1356-4 (pdf).—
ISBN 978-1-4598-1357-1 (epub)

1. Christmas—Juvenile literature. I. Tate-Stratton, Danielle, 1987–,
author II. Title. III. Series: Orca origins
GT4985.5.T38 2018   j394.2663   C2017-907692-2
C2017-907693-0

First published in the United States, 2018
Library of Congress Control Number: 2018933729

Summary: Part of the nonfiction Origins series for middle readers. Illustrated with archival and color photographs, the book looks at the history and practice of Christmas celebrations around the globe.

Orca Book Publishers is dedicated to preserving the environment and has printed this book on Forest Stewardship Council® certified paper.

Orca Book Publishers gratefully acknowledges the support for its publishing programs provided by the following agencies: the Government of Canada through the Canada Book Fund and the Canada Council for the Arts, and the Province of British Columbia through the BC Arts Council and the Book Publishing Tax Credit.

The authors and publisher have made every effort to ensure that the information in this book was correct at the time of publication. The authors and publisher do not assume any liability for any loss, damage or disruption caused by errors or omissions. Every effort has been made to trace copyright holders and to obtain their permission for the use of copyright material. The publisher apologizes for any errors or omissions in the above list and would be grateful if notified of any corrections that should be incorporated in future reprints or editions of this book.

Edited by Sarah N. Harvey
Designed by Rachel Page
Front cover photos by SWNS.com, Stocksy.com, iStock.com, Unsplash.com.
Back cover photo by Stocksy.com

ORCA BOOK PUBLISHERS
orcabook.com

Printed and bound in Canada.

21 20 19 18 • 4 3 2 1

For Helga, who never compromised when it came to Christmas.
—NT

For Peta, who understands the pleasures of coordinated wrapping paper,
early planning, activity Advent calendars and, most important, time spent with family;
you're my kindred Christmas Spirit! I can't wait to celebrate many,
many more crazy family Christmases with you!
—DTS

CONTENTS

Chapter Three:
Celebrations around the World

Choosing just the right Christmas tree makes for a fun expedition for the whole family.
Stocksy.com

Each year we put our tree up on December 10, my father's birthday. Decorating the tree marks the official beginning of our family's Christmas season. (NT)

INTRODUCTION

In our family, it's hard to imagine what December would be like without a Christmas celebration. Until we began the research for this book, we didn't know exactly why we always decorate a Christmas tree, light a fire in our fireplace and leave a tray of milk and cookies outside on Christmas Eve. We sing *carols* that celebrate the birth of Jesus Christ, as well as those that feature characters like Frosty the Snowman and Rudolph the Red-Nosed Reindeer. Some of the traditions we follow date back thousands of years, while others, like watching a festive movie, are more modern. Sorting out where our various traditions originated led us to discover that although we celebrate and understand Christmas in one way, there are many interpretations of what is the best and most appropriate way to honor the season.

Nikki doesn't dress up too often, but the tradition of putting on a nice outfit at Christmas began in childhood and continues today. Here, Nikki and her cousin celebrate Christmas in England in 1967.

Helga Williams

Not all Christmases include snow. Our family has celebrated on the beaches of Australia, Florida, California and Hawaii, depending on where we lived at the time.

Stocksy.com

ONE

Season of Darkness, Season of Light

A midwinter celebration held in December and January is common in many parts of the world. That's true even when, in places like Australia, the "winter" months fall during the hottest part of the year. Why do so many people in the world embrace festivities that include such features as a baby in a manger, a jolly old man in red, a grinchy tightwad, gifts, indoor trees and a stuffed turkey on the dinner table—all in the name of Christmas? Let's take a look at where all those midwinter celebrations began.

Early Midwinter Celebrations

In the depths of winter, when the days are short and the temperatures are chilly, it's not surprising that people look

Ancient Egyptian sun god Ra.
Vladimir Zadvinskii/Shutterstock.com

forward to the long warm days of spring and summer. Thousands of years ago, when winter could be a time of fear, discomfort and starvation, the promise of the sun's eventual return was certainly worth celebrating.

In the **northern hemisphere**, the shortest day of the year is December 21 or 22 (winter **solstice**), after which each day gets a little longer until June 21 or 22 (summer solstice), the day each year with the most hours of daylight. In the northernmost towns, people must endure nearly twenty-four hours of darkness on that shortest, darkest day.

Midwinter celebrations were common throughout the northern hemisphere long before Christian leaders adopted December 25 as a special holy day. (And yes, that's the origin of the word *holiday.*)

Many ancient peoples, like the Egyptians, worshipped the sun or had sun gods. Ancient structures such as the Egyptian pyramids were sometimes built to align with the sun's position on certain special days. The solstice was just one of the things that was celebrated, along with birthdays and key planting and harvest dates.

The Norse word for a midwinter season of celebration is *Jul* (*Jól* in Iceland). The English word *yule* may come from these Nordic roots. In Old Norse poetry, the word was sometimes used to mean "feast." Today the word generally refers to the Christmas holiday season.

Time to Feast

Midwinter was a good time for feasting because livestock, like lambs born in spring, had often reached a good size for slaughter. With food being hard to find at that time of year, it made sense to feast on meat rather than to keep feeding livestock when hay and grain were more expensive. Fermented ales and fruit wines were also ready to drink about then, and alcohol was often part of the partying that took place during solstice festivals.

Yule Logs and the Yule Goat

The **yule log** is a large piece of wood that people put in their fireplaces at Christmas. Sometimes yule logs were burned until there was nothing left but ashes. The ashes were collected after the log was gone and were spread in gardens and fields. (Adding ash to the soil provides some nutrients and can help certain plants grow better.)

Christmas Unwrapped

High-Tech Yule Logs

Today, it's possible to enjoy the tradition of the yule log even if you don't have a fireplace, as long as you have a television or computer. In 1966, the television station WPIX broadcast footage of a burning log for three hours on Christmas Eve, for New Yorkers who didn't have a fireplace. The original film was shot at Gracie Mansion, where the mayor of New York City lives. Filming was a little more exciting than anyone expected. To get a clear shot of the burning fire, the film crew removed the safety screen. A spark flew out of the fireplace and set an expensive antique rug on fire! The original yule log film lasted only 17 seconds and was looped over and over while it was aired.

Because the program was so popular, it was refilmed a few years later in California and was then rebroadcast for 23 years. (The new version was 6 minutes long and was a little less jerky.) Many imitations have since been created and shown on various television stations and over the Internet, and recorded on DVDs, including one that stars various cast members from the animated film *Shrek*.

The French made sure to keep some yule log ashes for tucking under beds, as the ashes were thought to keep nasty storms away over the year ahead.

In Scandinavia, there were many beliefs and traditions relating to the autumn harvest. One was that the last sheaf of straw of the harvest had magical properties, and it was saved and kept for the Yule celebrations. One of the important gods of the harvest feasts was Thor, who was believed to control weather and storms. One theory is that the straw bundles were shaped into a goat because Thor was said to have two goats. Although these straw goats were originally related to harvest festivals, today the yule goat (*julebok* in Swedish, *julebukk* in Norwegian and *joulupukki* in Finnish) has become a symbol of Christmas.

In Nordic countries, yule goats made of straw are associated with the Christmas season.
cenglanddesigns/iStock.com

Ancient Rome

Farther south, the pre-Christian Romans were very good at partying—especially at midwinter. As far back as 217 **BCE** (before the Common Era), there are records of ancient Romans celebrating *Saturnalia*, a festival honoring Saturn, the god of seeds and prosperity. There was feasting, drinking, gambling and general rowdiness for seven days, from December 17 to 23, during which only people who prepared food were allowed to work. Schools and courts were closed, wars halted and disagreements between citizens put on hold. Slaves and their masters briefly exchanged roles. Homes were decorated with greenery, and people exchanged gifts of candles and clay dolls. Fruit was meant to bring good luck and encourage fertility. Dolls were not toys to be played with, as they are today, but symbols of human sacrifice.

The Roman Forum and ruins of the Septimius Severus Arch and the Saturn Temple in Rome, Italy.
melis/Shutterstock.com

Ancient Greece

Ancient Greeks celebrated an important midwinter festival of their own, this one the birth of Dionysus in December. Said to be the divine son of Zeus (the king of the ancient Greek gods) and a human woman named Semele, Dionysus was the youngest god to be welcomed to Olympus, home of the Greek gods. Carols—songs that were once tied closely to dances—were sung to honor the rebirth of Dionysus. It was believed that Dionysus was born twice—once by his human mother and once after he emerged from where he had been sewn into his father's leg. Children sang these songs while visiting rich people's homes.

December 26, the day after Christmas, is a holiday in many places. It is known as Boxing Day in Canada and other Commonwealth countries, and St. Stephen's Day in most European countries. One theory is that the boxes may refer to a **Middle Ages** tradition of workers asking for tips (in a box) for good service.

13

2.500 ΕΤΗ ΘΕΑΤΡΟΥ - ΑΡΜΑ ΘΕΣΠΙΔΟΣ

ΕΛΛΑΣ - HELLAS ΔΡ. 1.50

Dionysus in his chariot.
Lefteris Papaulakis/Shutterstock.com

Flying Chariots

The idea of someone being pulled on a flying vehicle towed by animals has been around for a long time. In ancient Greece, Dionysus got around in a chariot pulled by various flying creatures, including panthers, tigers, stags, bulls or gryphons (creatures with the body of a lion and the head and wings of an eagle). Thor's chariot was pulled by two goats. In Norse mythology, a horse pulled the sun god across the sky, an idea similar to that found in the Vedic religion of northwestern India. It's quite possible that centuries later, artists and illustrators who were wondering what Santa's mode of transportation might look like were inspired by earlier depictions of some of these earlier flying chariots.

Early Christianity

According to Christian tradition, around 3 or 4 BCE, in Israel, a baby named Jesus was born in a stable. He became a preacher with a large following, and his teachings formed the foundation for a new religion called **Christianity**. The celebration of his birth would eventually become a midwinter celebration, today observed by more than two billion people around the world.

The Story of the Nativity

The story of Jesus's birth is known as the **Nativity**. It is described in two places in the **New Testament**, the part of the Bible written by various authors during the

This stained-glass window in a cathedral in Brussels, Belgium, depicts the Nativity.
jorisvo/Shutterstock.com

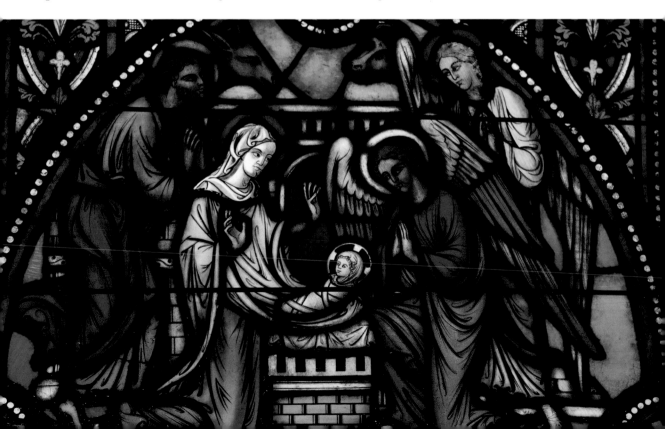

A crèche with figurines including Jesus, Mary, Joseph, sheep and Magi.
ANDROMACHI/Shutterstock.com

Christmas Unwrapped

December 25

No one knows the actual date of Jesus's birth as it was never mentioned in the Bible. So why do we celebrate Christmas on December 25? The answer to that question is a very long story, and scholars have argued about it for about 2,000 thousand years. Christmas probably wasn't celebrated much at all for almost 300 years after Jesus was born. And December 25 wasn't chosen by the Christian church as the date until around the middle of the fourth century CE, a few years after Christians were allowed to practice their religion legally.

Some scholars believe that December 25 was chosen because it was nine months after an angel told Mary that she would become the mother of Jesus. Others think the Christians wanted to make use of the non-Christian festival declared in 273 CE as the official day to celebrate the Roman sun god known as Sol Invictus, or the Unconquered Sun. (In early Christianity, the sun was often used as a symbol for Jesus.) Another theory proposes that the church decided to make Jesus's official birthday coincide with the existing festival of Saturnalia. What is clear is that December 25 became known as the Feast of the Nativity, and much later as "Christmas" (or "Christ's Mass").

first century **CE** (Common Era). The Gospel of Luke tells the story of Mary and Joseph traveling to Bethlehem to register for the Roman census. After Mary gave birth in a stable, an angel spoke to shepherds who were watching over their sheep and told them that the son of God had been born. The Gospel of Matthew describes the Star of Bethlehem and how its light led the Magi (also known as the three wise men or the three kings) and their gifts of gold, *frankincense* and **myrrh** to the stable in Bethlehem, where they found the baby Jesus in a manger. Once the date of Jesus's birth was settled on December 25 (see sidebar), a number of other important dates in the Christian calendar were set as well.

To remember this important story, many people have a crèche—a miniature version of the Nativity scene—among their indoor or outdoor Christmas decorations. Crèches often include a stable with animals, hay and a tiny baby in a manger. The first Nativity scene is thought to have been staged in 1223, when St. Francis of Assisi organized a scene including a live ox and a donkey in Grecio, an Italian hill town. As villagers came by to examine the Nativity scene, St. Francis preached about the birth of baby Jesus. Although some of the words were in Latin, some were also sung in Italian, the language of the audience. As time went on, Nativity scenes became more elaborate and came to include additional characters.

Early Christians believed that the Magi arrived to find the baby Jesus on January 6, which they called **Epiphany**. They also believed it to be the day on which Jesus was later baptized and in following years performed two important miracles. In the West, Epiphany celebrated the Magi, the three kings who had brought gifts for the baby. It became a day of gift giving, and children in many parts of the world still receive gifts from the three kings on January 6.

Frankincense and myrrh are both resins from trees that grow in Africa and the Middle East. They have been used for many purposes since ancient times, including being burned as incense in rituals and worship.

The Magi may have ridden camels on their journey to deliver gifts to the baby Jesus.
Shutterstock.com

Over the centuries, the Magi also became known as the three kings or three wise men. They were given a variety of names (the best known are Melchior, Gaspar and Balthasar). In fact, the Bible doesn't actually say how many Magi visited the baby Jesus in Bethlehem, and historians believe that the word **magi** referred to priests or astrologers from Persia.

The days between Christmas and Epiphany became known as the **Twelve Days of Christmas**. This festive time ended with **Twelfth Night**, a party that marked the end of the Christmas season. In many places, there was a special cake with a bean or other small item hidden in it. Whoever found the bean in his or her slice of cake got to be in charge of the festivities.

A special period called **Advent** preceded Christmas. In the West, Advent begins on the fourth Sunday before Christmas. For many centuries it was a time when people were supposed to prepare for the holiday by eating very little (or fasting) and avoiding games and other fun—as they do in the similar period before Easter known as Lent. Today, Advent is celebrated in many different ways around the world—for example, with **Advent calendars**. They have a little door for each day before Christmas, starting on December 1. Behind each door is a picture, a gift, candy or a chocolate. Other families light candles on

This unusual hanging Advent calendar has a small numbered gift for each day. The presents are displayed along with other seasonal decorations.
fotoknips/Shutterstock.com

an Advent wreath, which is made of evergreen boughs meant to symbolize everlasting life. The four candles on each wreath, each representing a week of Advent, are typically lit on Sundays, and a special prayer corresponding to each week may be said.

The Roman Empire officially adopted Christianity as its main religion in the fourth century CE. The established midwinter festivals and New Year's celebrations were so popular that many of the traditional practices blended in with Christian teachings, even though the church tried hard to get rid of them. In the next pages, we'll explore how some of these ancient practices can still be seen in Christmas celebrations around the world, together with modern practices that no one who lived 2,000 years ago could have dreamed of.

This Advent wreath features popular Christmas decorations like candles, evergreen branches, berries and holly leaves.
Magdalena Kucova/Shutterstock.com

At Christmas, the tree outside this church in Germany is decorated with lights.

Michael Thaler/Shutterstock.com

The Spread of Christianity

In the Middle Ages (between about 500 and 1500 CE) most people in Europe joined the Christian church. As Christianity spread, so did the tradition of celebrating the birth of Jesus on December 25. When Europeans traveled far and wide to explore the world and establish colonies, the Christian religion traveled along with them. Many midwinter traditions first seen in earlier times were used by the Christian church, and others were kept by people even when the church told them not to.

The Puritans

Taking place right alongside more serious services organized by the churches, many parts of Christmas celebrations were still attached to their rowdy pre-Christian roots. Loud and drunken groups sang and danced in the streets, eventually gathering outside the homes of the wealthy, demanding good food and wine, making lots of noise and threatening the homeowners if their wishes were not granted. Church leaders were not impressed.

By the seventeenth century, though, the church began to gain the upper hand. One group of Protestants, the **Puritans**, was so upset by the over-the-top frolicking that they canceled Christmas altogether during a period known as the Protestant Reformation. In 1647 Oliver Cromwell, a Puritan politician and soldier, made it illegal to celebrate Christmas in England. In 1659, the Puritan leaders in Massachusetts made it illegal to include Christmas in the church calendar.

Oliver Cromwell didn't just ban Christmas. He also closed many inns and theaters, forbade most nonreligious activities on Sundays, and made swearing and drunkenness illegal.
stu99/iStock.com

Christmas Unwrapped

The Protestant Reformation

Martin Luther, a professor and priest in Germany in the sixteenth century, objected to many policies and practices of the Roman Catholic Church. What bothered him most was that ordinary people paid the church to forgive their sins. Martin Luther believed that the forgiveness of sins could not be purchased, that it was a gift from God to those with faith. Many people liked Luther's ideas. The influence and popularity of the saints (including **Saint Nicholas**) declined, and a new form of Christianity, known as Protestantism, soon had many followers, including the Puritans.

The Puritans even frowned upon Christmas carols, so not many were written or sung in the 1600s and 1700s. However, there are some exceptions: "Hark the Herald Angels Sing" and "While Shepherds Watched Their Flocks by Night" were composed during that time.

Christmas Carols

Despite the best efforts of the church during certain time periods, Christmas carols were an important part of celebrating Christmas and continue to be. Religious and festive songs often accompanied dancing in ancient societies, including those of the Egyptians, Greeks, Romans and Celts. The word *carol* may have come from the Greek *chorus*, which was a circle dance. Although we sometimes refer to all Christmas songs as carols, a more precise definition is a song that celebrates the events or people of the Nativity.

Singing carols by candlelight.
PhotostockAR/Shutterstock.com

It's hard to say when the first Christmas carols were written, but one of the earliest carols that refers to the birth of Jesus ("*Jesus refulsit omnium*") was composed by St. Hilary of Poitiers in the fourth century CE.

Sometimes verses that existed several centuries ago were put to the music we are familiar with today many years after the original lyrics were written. For example, the words to "Adam Lay Ybounden" were written in the fifteenth century and set to music by the twentieth-century composer Benjamin Britten. The carol "Good King Wenceslas" is an example of the reverse: the melody is thought to date back to the thirteenth century, but the words were written and put to music by John Mason Neale in 1853. Many carols were composed in the fifteenth and sixteenth centuries, and quite a few of them are still sung today—for example, "I Saw Three Ships" and the German

Some Christmas carols are hundreds of years old. New Christmas music is written each year, but only some songs become classics that many people know.
1000 Words/Shutterstock.com

Christmas Unwrapped

Kisses Under the Mistletoe

Mistletoe is an unusual evergreen plant that produces its berries in winter, grows in trees and has no roots in the ground. It's not surprising that the ancient Europeans believed it had all kinds of special powers. They gathered and used it especially in midwinter. The tradition of kissing under the mistletoe is believed to have developed much later, though, in England. With each kiss, a berry was removed, until there were no more berries and the fun was over.

This mosaic of Saint Nicholas is in the Grgeteg Monastery in Fruška, Serbia.
Wikipedia

carol "O Tannenbaum" ("O Christmas Tree"). We'll look at some modern carols and songs in the next chapter.

Saint Nicholas

Saint Nicholas was a Turkish bishop in the fourth century. While little is known about his life, there are lots of wonderful legends about him. In one of these, he stood up to pray the moment he was born! Because of his miraculous powers and his kindness and generosity to children and the poor, Nicholas became a very popular saint, known best as the patron saint of children and sailors.

By the twelfth century, people throughout Europe had connected Saint Nicholas with Christmas. They celebrated his feast day, December 6 (the day on which he was believed to have died), by giving gifts to children. But during the Protestant Reformation, when celebrating saints was frowned upon, Saint Nicholas became less popular in much of Europe. The gift giving moved to Christmas Day, and in some places, for a time the giver was the baby Jesus himself, with various helpers.

Saint Nicholas continued to be important in the Netherlands, where he was known as Sinterklaas. Some Dutch people may have taken Sinterklaas with them when they immigrated to the United States, settling in what was to become New York City. Early in the nineteenth century, Sinterklaas became Santa Claus in the United States. (More about that in the next chapter). When Santa Claus was exported back to Europe, he became Father Christmas in England, Père Noël in France and the Weihnachtsmann in Germany.

Christmas Bounces Back

The Puritans may have tried their best to get rid of what they saw as an excuse for ungodly behavior, but as you can imagine, banning Christmas wasn't very popular. Many churchgoers continued to celebrate until the harsh laws were changed. After years of oppression, it took a while for Christmas to bounce back and for most churches to change their position.

In the 1800s, when many of the modern Christmas traditions we know and enjoy today were established, the celebrations were focused on children, families and good behavior. In the next chapter, we'll see how some of our seasonal festivities became popular.

CHRISTMAS CHERRY CAKE

This is my father-in-law's favorite recipe. White and red in color, this cake is perfect for Christmas. I'm sure Santa would enjoy a slice! (DTS)

Ingredients:

1 cup margarine or butter

2 cups white sugar

3 eggs, beaten

1 teaspoon lemon extract

3 cups all-purpose flour

1 teaspoon baking powder

1 teaspoon salt

¾ cup warm milk

1 teaspoon vanilla

2 cups glacé cherries, chopped

Directions:

Preheat oven to 325 degrees F. Line a baking tin with parchment paper. In a bowl, cream margarine and white sugar together well. Add eggs and lemon extract, mixing to combine. In a separate bowl, mix together flour, baking powder and salt. Add the dry mixture, alternating with the warm milk, to the first bowl, stirring to combine. Add the vanilla and stir. In the bowl used for the dry mixture, toss the chopped cherries in a little bit of flour to prevent them from clumping together, and stir cherries into the cake batter. Pour it into the prepared tin, cover tightly with tinfoil and bake for approximately 2 hours and 20 minutes. Check the cake for doneness after 90 minutes. Cake is done when a skewer inserted into the middle comes out clean.

Colin's Story

Nikki's English grandparents and their dog, Timothy, sit beside a tree lit with real candles, in the 1950s.

Colin Williams

Edward Colin Williams (Nikki's father and Dani's grandpa) was born in England in 1935, four years before the outbreak of World War II. Now in his eighties, Colin loves to talk about his childhood Christmases.

"Our small artificial tree was made of wire and tiny slivers of green paper 'pine needles.' It was lit with candles that sat in little metal clips that fastened to the branches." The tree's other decorations were simple—some glass balls and handmade paper ornaments hung among the candle-lit boughs. Although Colin recalls loving the way the tree looked, he rolls his eyes now when he thinks about the fire hazard his family cheerfully erected on the table each year. "We made paper garlands that we hung everywhere! That can't have been safe with all those candles!"

"Nobody had much during the war," he remembers. "And in the years after, everything was rationed." With money tight and few goods available to buy, families were creative when it came time to give presents.

"My father was very handy. He worked at the coal mine as a harness maker; he could make all sorts of things out of leather." Colin loved the leather cowboy hat and matching holster his father made for him, and he spent hours pretending to be a brave knight using a steel sword made by the local blacksmith.

"We always had a big dinner with a roast, lots of vegetables and Yorkshire puddings. My favorites were the brussels sprouts—I used to call them baby cabbages." It was hard to buy tropical fruit in England at the time, so it was a real treat when Colin would find an orange tucked into his Christmas stocking.

Baked treats like Christmas cake were always around during the holiday season, though Colin didn't like the icing. "Too sweet! I used to scrape that off, or my mother would make a plain Christmas cake just for me."

Thinking about singing carols, visiting family in nearby towns and villages and receiving special treats like chocolate still makes Colin smile. "We didn't have much," he says, "but we were very fortunate compared to so many others who had even less."

Christmas is still Colin's favorite time of year. Our family puts up the tree on December 10, Colin's birthday, just as his family did when he was a little boy. We always include brussels sprouts on the Christmas dinner table and make sure to have some icing-free Christmas cake on hand.

Colin wouldn't need to scrape the icing off this Christmas cake.
vm2002/Shutterstock.com

Nikki's Story

My brother Peter and I sing Christmas carols in front of the family tree around 1971. This was one tradition my mother insisted on keeping up through the years. (NT)

Helga Williams

When I was growing up, each year at Christmas my mother would sit at the piano and gather us around to sing Christmas carols. She knew how to play a great mix of the old traditional carols like "O Come All Ye Faithful" and "God Rest Ye Merry, Gentlemen," as well as more contemporary holiday songs like "White Christmas" and "Jingle Bells." Of the four children in my family, I was the only one who learned to play an instrument, the guitar. For a number of years before I left home and went off to do a bit of traveling and attend university, I played my guitar while Mom played the piano, and we all sang the carols we had learned.

Although my mother and I also belonged to several community choirs over the years, none of the other members of the family really enjoyed singing, and after my mother passed away the family carol-singing tradition changed. We don't sing together anymore, but we all love the music of the season, and Dani has amassed a great collection of Christmas music. From the time the tree goes up and is decorated until the day it comes down, Dani makes sure her Christmas playlist gets lots of airtime. We may not be singing together in a formal way, but it's pretty well impossible to be in our house and not start humming along.

Singing carols together is one of the ways
that people celebrate the Christmas season.

Ronnie Comeau/Stocksy.com

Santa statue on a street in the Netherlands.
Stocksy.com

TWO

THE BEGINNINGS OF MODERN CHRISTMAS

Christmas may have had its roots in ancient midwinter festivals and then been blended with Christian teachings, but many of the traditions we associate with the holiday season today were invented quite recently.

Saint Nicholas, Meet Santa Claus!

In his 1809 book *Diedrich Knickerbocker's History of New York*, the American author Washington Irving jokingly described Saint Nicholas as the beloved patron of the Dutch colonists. But most of the colonists had been Puritans who had long since left Saint Nick behind. Their descendants were not pleased with Irving. But the details he created are still familiar today, such as Saint Nicholas

Nikki as a child with Santa.
Helga Williams

The first printed reference to "Santeclaus" using a flying reindeer to help deliver presents was in a children's book published in 1821 called The Children's friend: A New-Year's Present, to Little Ones from Five to Twelve. The author and illustrator are both unknown, but like "The Night Before Christmas," the book played a major role in shaping the Santa Claus of today.

Santa and Mrs. Claus dolls on display at a Christmas market in Riga, Latvia.
bruev/iStock.com

using a flying wagon and climbing down chimneys to deliver presents to children, smoking a pipe and laying a finger beside his nose.

In 1810 fellow New Yorker John Pintard, a historian and founder of the New-York Historical Society, published a pamphlet that included a pair of images: the first of Saint Nicholas as a serious bishop, the second of children with gifts (treats for the girl, sticks for the naughty boy) standing near stockings hung by a cheery fire. Pintard's pamphlet helped introduce Americans to Saint Nicholas and encouraged the idea of families celebrating Christmas Eve and Christmas Day together at home.

A few years later, in about 1822, a serious professor and poet named Clement Clarke Moore had a bit of fun and, legend has it, composed a lighthearted poem for his children on Christmas Eve, after picking up a Christmas turkey. The next day he read it to his family. Originally titled "A Visit from St. Nicholas," the poem is now more commonly known as "The Night before Christmas."

GOD JUL!

Although a family friend sent the poem off for publication in 1823, Moore didn't admit to being its author until he included it in a book of his poems published in 1844. Clement Clarke Moore didn't intend to completely change the way people thought about Christmas, but his poem played an important part in turning Christmas into a celebration that centered on children.

Several artists came up with illustrations to go along with Moore's poem, but it wasn't until 1863, when a German immigrant named Thomas Nast started publishing his drawings of Saint Nick in *Harper's Illustrated Weekly* each year at Christmas, that our modern idea of what Santa looks like was born. Nast's imagination was also responsible for providing Santa Claus with his North Pole address, as well as the famous book in which he keeps track of how children behave during the year.

This Christmas-card image was created by the Swedish painter and illustrator Adèle Söderberg, who lived in Stockholm in the late 1800s and early 1900s.
Wikimedia.com

Charles Dickens in his study.
kreicher/iStock.com

Rich and Poor

In 1843, the English author Charles Dickens was going through a tough time. His writing was not selling well, and he was having trouble paying his bills and taking care of his growing family. (At the time, he had four children, and his wife was pregnant with their fifth.) Dickens had grown up in poverty and knew firsthand the terrible conditions for the poor in England. Children and orphans started their working lives as young as the age of three, eventually working up to eighteen hours a day in the coal mines and giving what little money they earned to their parents or the orphanages where they lived.

It seemed that the wealthy members of society didn't really care about the dreadful situation, and many were unwilling to do anything about it. Hoping to draw attention to the plight of children living in poverty—and relieve his own financial worries—Dickens wrote *A Christmas Carol*. An instant success, the story has come to represent the true meaning of Christmas.

Modern Christmas Music

In chapter 1 we looked at how some of the oldest carols came to be and how singing them fell out of favor for a couple of hundred years during the Protestant Reformation. In the 1800s, old carols were dug out and dusted off, and a new round of carol composition took place. Chances are you know the words to some of the most famous American carols composed at about this time, like "We Three Kings of Orient Are" (1857) and "O Little Town of Bethlehem" (1868). The popular sleighing song "Jingle Bells" was composed around 1851 by an American musician named James Pierpont.

In Cornwall, England, Edward Benson, who would later become the Archbishop of Canterbury, organized a series of religious readings and carols to be performed on Christmas Eve in 1880. Other churches began to use the service, which became known as *A Festival of Nine Lessons and Carols*. It became famous after World War I when the choir of King's College at Cambridge Univeristy in England performed it in the order of the readings and carols still heard most often today.

Christmas Unwrapped

Follow That Sleigh!

Sometimes a Christmas tradition has its beginnings in pure chance. Such was the case with NORAD's Santa Tracker. Each year, the North American Aerospace Defense Command (NORAD) publishes information about Santa's exact whereabouts, a tradition that began by accident in 1955.

A common version of the story is that on November 30 a child who wanted to tell Santa Claus that she would be leaving out some food for both him and his reindeer, and to let him know what was on her wish list, dialed the wrong number. (It was a misprint in an advertisement.) Instead of Santa, she reached the desk of Colonel Harry Shoup, at what was then known as the US Continental Air Defense Command. The colonel then told his staff to answer calls and provide updates on the exact coordinates of Santa's sleigh as it traveled from the North Pole and around the world, delivering presents.

Today, information provided by NORAD on Christmas Eve is spread widely through the media, online at a special website and through an app. Volunteers answer emails and take phone calls, talking to children all over the world who have questions about Santa's progress.

The opening verse of the first carol, "Once in Royal David's City," is sung by one of the younger boys in the choir. Several boys are trained to sing the opening melody, but the one who is chosen to perform on Christmas Eve is told only moments before the service begins. The performance has been broadcast on the BBC each year since 1928 and for many people is an important part of Christmas.

Several well-known, playful Christmas tunes were written in the United States in the twentieth century, though for reasons you might not expect. In 1939 Robert Lewis May wrote a poem about Rudolph, an unhappy reindeer who was bullied by his reindeer friends, for a free booklet that the Montgomery Ward department store would give to its customers at Christmas. The booklets were a hit, and the company gave away millions of them in the 1940s. In 1949 May's brother-in-law, the

Christmas carolers outside St. Ann's Church in downtown Dublin, Ireland.
JannHuizenga/iStock.com

Reindeer ornaments for the Christmas tree come in all shapes and sizes.
jayfish/iStock.com

One of the world's best-known carols was composed on Christmas Eve in 1818, when a rusty old organ at an Austrian church could not be played for the midnight service. The local priest, Father Joseph Mohr, had written the words to "Stille Nacht" ("Silent Night") two years before, and he asked the church organist, Franz Gruber, to compose a simple melody for the poem on a guitar. The new carol was ready in time for the service at midnight.

songwriter Johnny Marks, changed the poem to lyrics for a song and set them to music. (He also wrote "Rockin' around the Christmas Tree" in 1958 and "A Holly Jolly Christmas" in 1964.) Country music and TV star Gene Autry sang the song, which shot to the top of the charts, and Rudolph became one of the best-known characters of the Christmas season. He has been featured in subsequent books, which have been translated into other languages, and a movie, and "his" song has been recorded by dozens of singers and musicians.

The following year, Walter E. "Jack" Rollins and Steve Nelson wrote "Frosty the Snowman." It was again performed by Gene Autry and has been a popular song during the holidays ever since. Frosty also starred in several television specials, the first of which came out in 1969.

The World's Largest Christmas Store

Wally Bronner, who founded the self-proclaimed "Largest Christmas Store in the World" in 1954, fell into the Christmas-decoration trade quite by accident. At age 16 he started a successful sign-painting business in his parents' basement. A few years later some store owners in Clare, Michigan, wanted Christmas decorations for their town's lampposts. After painting custom signs for them, Bronner realized there could be a market for holiday decorations, and he opened the first version of his shop in 1954. Bronner built the business with his wife, Irene, purchasing three additional buildings to contain their ever-growing stock, before opening the enormous Bronner's at its current location, 25 Christmas Lane, Frankenmuth, Michigan, in 1977.

The current building covers the area of five and a half football fields (almost seven and a half acres) and stocks 50,000 types of Christmas ornaments and decorations! Not just your typical glass baubles, the ornaments represent just about every profession—including dog groomer—as well as various sports and locations across the United States (and around the world). There's even a category specifically for ornaments featuring s'mores!

Dani and Toryn cut down this massive tree, which took hours to decorate.
Nikki Tate

Christmas Trees

Greenery was an important part of many pre-Christian midwinter celebrations, a symbol of the growing season that would eventually return. No one is quite sure when trees were first used as part of Christmas celebrations. One theory is that the Christmas tree evolved from the "paradise tree," the main prop in a popular mystery play in the Middle Ages telling the story of Creation from the Bible. The tree, often a fir tree, was decorated with apples to represent the Garden of Eden. When the plays were no longer performed, people may have decorated their own paradise trees on December 24, the feast day of Adam and Eve.

The first records of decorated Christmas trees in Germany are from the 1600s. Tree decorations included roses (symbols of the Virgin Mary), apples, wafers, candies, sugar lumps and, finally, in 1660, candles.

Another German ancestor of the Christmas tree was a decoration known as a pyramid. Made of wood, these multilevel carousels were about a meter and a half (five feet) high. At the top, a propeller mounted on a rotating shaft turned as heat rose from candles placed on the shelves below. Nativity scenes, angels, greenery, fruits and vegetables decorated the various levels. The pyramid tradition spread to Italy and England and then, with German immigrants in the early 1700s, to North America.

Written descriptions of trees festooned with ornaments, gifts and candles appeared in North America in the early 1800s, and the first illustration of a decorated tree appeared in 1836 in a book called *The Stranger's Gift*.

This gigantic Christmas pyramid is on display at the Christmas market in Bad Salzuflen, Germany.
Bastian Sande/Shutterstock.com

Perhaps the biggest boost to the Christmas tree's popularity came in 1848 when an illustration of Queen Victoria, her German husband, Albert, and several of their children appeared in the *London Illustrated News.* The picture showed the tree lit with candles, hung with edible decorations and topped by an angel, with presents underneath. A similar illustration was published two years later, and from then on a decorated tree was considered an essential part of Christmas decor. Because the upper classes read more than those with less education, the obsession with bigger and fancier trees started with wealthy families, but the Christmas tree was soon adopted by families from all social classes.

In 1870 German artisans started exporting fancy handmade glass decorations. Today whole shops specialize in

For many families, decorating the tree is a special part of the Christmas season.
iStock.com

Here's a green way to take the tree home!
iStock.com

nothing but Christmas ornaments! A big change in the way trees were decorated came in 1882 when Edward Johnson, who worked with inventor Thomas Edison, created the first string of electric tree lights. These were much safer than candles and over time replaced the open flames.

The first decorated Christmas tree appeared inside the White House in 1889, and the first official national Christmas tree was set up there in 1929. The First Lady, Lou Henry Hoover, started the tradition of the president's wife being in charge of decorating the tree. While having the national Christmas tree in the White House is now a well-established tradition, in the years between 1889 and 1929 it wasn't without controversy. For example, in 1899 some people even wrote to President William McKinley's office suggesting that having a Christmas tree in the

White House was "un-American," since it was originally a German custom.

In 1931 construction workers put up a six-meter (twenty-foot) tree in the muddy construction site of the future Rockefeller Center, a complex of nineteen buildings that would eventually cover nine hectares (twenty-two acres) in New York City. This began a tradition: every year thousands of visitors admire a beautifully decorated tree, and the official light-up is broadcast live on NBC. The trees are often donated and have come from as far away as Ottawa, Ontario. In 2015 a couple living in Gardiner, New York, realized they would have to remove an eighty-year-old, twenty-four-meter (seventy-eight-foot) spruce from their property because it was at risk of falling on their home. Instead of going through with the original plan, which was to chop it up for a whole lot of firewood,

Al Asendorf and Nancy Puchalski offered it to the Rockefeller Center, where it had an impressive second life as New York's most famous tree.

Gift Giving

The gifts of gold, frankincense and myrrh presented to the baby Jesus in Bethlehem by the Magi are often thought of as the first Christmas presents. It's not clear exactly when Christians began to celebrate the Nativity with gift giving, but over the centuries gifts were given on various dates in the Christmas season by various givers, including Saint Nicholas, the three kings and the baby Jesus himself.

The exchange of gifts we know it today didn't really start until the 1700s, when Christmas gifts began to be

Joel R. Poinsett first brought the plants that are now so popular as seasonal decorations to the United States in 1828. Native to Mexico and Central America, poinsettias bloom at Christmas. The red and white plants are also known as Christmas Star.

The three kings bring gifts to the baby Jesus.
Regien Paassen/Shutterstock.com

Christmas in the App Age

I love buying presents even more than I love receiving them, and I've been known to start my Christmas shopping during the after-Christmas sales of the year before. By May I'm well on my way to having purchased presents for many of the people on my list, and in many years I've completely finished shopping by October. One problem I have just about every year, though, is forgetting what I have already bought, especially if I wrapped it several months earlier! While it can be fun to be surprised right along with the recipient, I'm always worried I'll forget a long-wrapped gift in the back of a closet and won't even realize it's missing from under the tree. Recently I upgraded my Santa capabilities with a smartphone app called Santa's Bag. It allows you to keep track of all the details about your Christmas shopping, including where you've hidden the gifts. (DTS)

advertised. In the early 1800s, gift books were specially created collections of stories, essays and poetry that came out in time for the Christmas season. *Forget Me Not: A Christmas and New Year's Present for 1823* was the first of these books to be published in English. It was so successful that publishers began to produce others that were intended to be given to ladies. Soon, though, special editions were also published for children.

By the time the poem "The Night before Christmas" was being widely read and was believed to reflect the way Christmas was meant to be celebrated, expectations had changed, and most family members (especially children) looked forward to seeing what gifts they would receive each year. As the nineteenth century came to a close, Christmas shopping to provide all those expected gifts had become as much a part of the holiday season as singing carols or decorating trees.

Let's Shop! (or Not)

In some places where the season's festive connections are not rooted in history or religion, Christmas has been embraced as a commercial holiday, much like Valentine's Day or Halloween have become opportunities to sell cards, chocolates or costumes.

With the advent of new traditions such as Black Friday, where stores open on midnight the Friday after American Thanksgiving (the fourth Thursday in November), the Christmas season—for some people—has become all about buying stuff. Shoppers may wait for hours to snap up the perfect deal, and sometimes get pushed, shoved or even trampled in the process.

For others, this over-the-top consumerism is not what Christmas should be about. Some people are moving away from a gift-based idea of Christmas altogether. Eager to avoid the stress and expense of buying so many gifts, some families embrace ideas like making a present for each member of the family or donating money to charity in honor of the gift recipient.

In the final chapter, we will learn more about how cultures around the world celebrate Christmas.

At our house each year, family members of all ages help decorate a gingerbread house.
Nikki Tate

GINGERBREAD BARS

We love the taste of gingerbread, so there are always gingery baked goods around.
For spicier bars, double the amount of cinnamon, cloves and ginger.

Ingredients:

¾ cup margarine or butter
2 cups all-purpose flour
1 cup white sugar
2 teaspoons baking soda
1 teaspoon cinnamon
½ teaspoon cloves
½ teaspoon ginger
½ teaspoon salt
1 egg
¼ cup molasses
2 tablespoons white sugar

Directions:

Heat oven to 375 degrees F. Grease a 10-by-15-inch jelly-roll pan. Melt margarine in the microwave in a microwaveable bowl or on the stovetop in a large saucepan. Cool it for 1 to 2 minutes. Add the remaining ingredients, except 2 table-spoons white sugar, and mix well. Press batter into the pan, spreading evenly, and then sprinkle with remaining white sugar. Bake for 10 to 12 minutes. Let stand for 5 minutes, cut into bars and cool completely. Makes 48 bars.

Dani's Story

Christmas lights in Japan (like this display in Kobe) are nothing short of spectacular.

tera.ken/Shutterstock.com

When I moved to Japan, I expected Christmas to be more low-key than it is at home. I certainly didn't expect the decorations to be fancier than they are in Canada! Many train stations, shopping areas, outdoor spaces and department stores put up elaborate decorations for Christmas. One of my favorite things to do was walk around and look at the amazing lights on the way home from work. Winter light displays, which can include millions of lights all over trees, buildings and even the ground, are real tourist attractions in many towns, and I used to look through special guides to decide where to go to gaze in awe at the displays (some of which included 3-D laser shows!).

While some things in Japan were even more Christmasy than at home, others were definitely more of a challenge! It's really hard to cook a proper Christmas dinner in a kitchen without a full-size oven. Many Japanese stoves have only two small burners and a fish grill, so the magazine that I worked for always published articles about cooking a modified Christmas dinner in a typical Japanese kitchen.

One year, I went to visit my friend who lived in military housing, where we had access to an American-style grocery store and could buy flour and icing at reasonable prices. (Baking in Japan is expensive! I once spent fifty dollars on ingredients for just one carrot cake.) We spent the whole afternoon making Christmas cookie dough, which I then took to my uncle's house to bake, since he was the only person I knew who had an oven. Not wanting to carry all of the dough on the train, I sent it by courier, or *takkyubin*, which is a system of delivery so efficient it would make Santa jealous! For about ten dollars I managed to send enough dough for 150 cookies, in a refrigerated truck, all the way across town (about seventy kilometers, or forty-four miles). It arrived just a few hours after I did. I used the dough for a decorate-your-cookie party that I hosted. I invited all my friends to come over, watch Christmas movies from my childhood and have a taste of a Canadian Christmas. Since we didn't have a Christmas tree, I decorated a large palm tree in the living room.

One of the hardest things about living abroad is not being able to go home for Christmas. My boss at the time, a British woman who had lived in Tokyo for about a decade, dedicated herself to making Christmas the very best day she could for her friends and co-workers who couldn't go home. With a basket of Santa hats by the door, in case you had forgotten your own, and five Christmas trees scattered around the house (including a small one on the fridge), her legendary feasts required nearly a year of planning. I remember looking at our office calendar one day in October and smiling when I saw a note saying it was time to start the pickled onions for dinner on Christmas Day.

My years spent in Tokyo were made extra special by everyone I knew going out of their way to help others find their feet during the holidays and ensure that no one was left to celebrate alone. It was a spirit of Christmas—and community—that I truly cherished.

A Lump of Concrete: Best Present Ever!

Sometimes the most meaningful gifts of all have little or no monetary value. After World War II, Germany was divided into two countries: East Germany (the German Democratic Republic) became part of the Soviet Union and West Germany remained an independent nation. For many years a large wall divided the city of Berlin, which had sections belonging to each of the two countries. In some cases, family members found themselves living on opposite sides of the divided country. This happened to my mother's family, and for decades she believed she would never see a day when the wall would come down.

In 1989 political changes in Eastern Europe led to the border between East and West Germany being opened, and over the next several years the Berlin Wall was dismantled. When one of my brothers visited Berlin, he picked up a piece of wall that had been broken off during the deconstruction process. He wrapped it up and put it under the Christmas tree that year, and when my mother opened the package she burst into tears of joy. That lump of concrete with its faded graffiti paint was one of the Christmas gifts she treasured most. (NT)

The star is a symbol of light and also a reminder that a bright star over Bethlehem is said to have guided the three wise men to the stable where Jesus was born.

THREE

CELEBRATIONS AROUND THE WORLD

Although Christmas as we know it today may have its roots in Europe, the celebration has traveled far and wide. In this chapter we'll explore how people in different countries make merry during the holiday season. Even in our own family we've seen how Christmas traditions change over time and as our family has moved from place to place.

Light

In the northern hemisphere, Christmas takes place close to the winter solstice, when the nights are longest. It's not surprising that light is an important part of Christmas decorations. In Greenland, for example, which is so far

Where Christmas Is Welcome, and Where It's Not

Over 160 countries celebrate Christmas in some form. In some places, it's a holiday only for people who identify as Christian. But in many other places, different beliefs coexist, and often blend, in ways that result in unusual festivities. In Thailand, for example, you may see elephants wearing Santa suits during the holiday season!

In some countries today, though, the celebration of Christmas is not encouraged. In Saudi Arabia, for example, the official state religion is Islam, and devout Muslims are not supposed to indulge in Christmas festivities. Other countries with strict rules about which religious holidays are to be observed (and that do not officially sanction Christmas) include North Korea, Tajikistan and Brunei.

north that in the heart of winter the sun never rises, a popular decoration is a lit star in the window of each house—a small way to bring some light and cheer to the community.

Even in the **southern hemisphere**, where Christmas happens at midsummer instead of midwinter, light is an important part of Christmas celebrations. In Argentina, for example, the sky gets decorated on Christmas Eve! It is common to "toast" the beginning of Christmas Day by setting off fireworks at midnight. Many people set off fireworks on their own, and the skies fill with bright, colorful lights as the streets become crowded with tired children and their families watching the spectacle and calling *Feliz Navidad* to each other.

Christmas fireworks are part of Christmas celebrations in many places and in both hemispheres.
emarto/iStock.com

Something else you might see in Argentina's night sky late on Christmas Eve are *globos*, colorful paper lanterns with small candles inside them. The rising hot air allows the lanterns to magically float off into the sky.

In Argentina, when thousands of paper lanterns float up together, it is a beautiful sight.
iStock.com

Feasting

One of the highlights of the Christmas season is at least one special meal—on Christmas Eve or Christmas Day—or special foods eaten throughout the festive season. Whether it is the turkey dinner with all the trimmings that we are accustomed to in North America or the decomposed seal-skin-and-auk combo favored in Greenland, special meals are a sure sign of festive days. Sitting around the table with family and friends is one of the most common ways in which Christmas is celebrated around the world.

In many places, Christmas meals revolve around meat, and today turkey is often the meat of choice—even in England, where for centuries people enjoyed a Christmas goose. But don't get the idea that all Christmas dinners must be the same! There are almost as many ways of cooking Christmas turkeys as there are countries: turkey can be marinated, soaked in salt water and stuffed with everything from rice to truffles to chestnuts. In Mexico, the turkey might be served with a *mole* sauce made from chili peppers and chocolate.

For many people in Japanese cities, the fowl on the Christmas menu is chicken, and one of the most popular places to eat it is Kentucky Fried Chicken! In the weeks

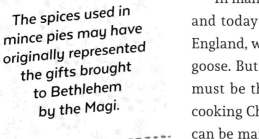

The spices used in mince pies may have originally represented the gifts brought to Bethlehem by the Magi.

A Christmas dinner in Japan will often include fried chicken.

iStock.com

leading up to Christmas, models of Colonel Sanders, which stand outside the shops year-round, are dressed up as Santa, and a special holiday menu is introduced. Perhaps as a result of an advertising campaign from way back in 1974 (which featured the slogan "Kentucky for Christmas"), KFC is eaten in over 3.5 million homes on or around Christmas every year. To handle the demand, KFC restaurants start accepting holiday-season reservations as early as October!

In Zimbabwe, too, chicken is a special Christmas treat and is often served with rice. Chicken is too expensive for many families to have on a regular basis, so it is reserved for this special festive meal.

Other meats may form the Christmas centerpiece too. In Greece, pork is the traditional Christmas fare.

Santa hats, sparklers, Christmas crackers and lots of great food are regular features of our family Christmas gatherings.
iStock.com

Fufu, made from plantains, yams or the starchy roots of the cassava plant, is a popular dish in western and central Africa.

eatsmarter_de/iStock.com

In Greenland, the big seasonal treat is *kiviak*, the flesh of an auk (a small seabird) that has been buried for several months in a sealskin and left until fully decomposed—a local delicacy!

In Ghana, one of the traditional Christmas dishes is a special soup that includes various types of meat, including chopped African land snails. If the idea of consuming a giant gastropod doesn't whet your appetite, *fufu*, a dish made from pounded cassava, is also commonly served.

Christmas meals may also be meatless or feature fish instead of meat. In several Central and Eastern European countries, the traditional Christmas Eve dinner consists of twelve courses. In Ukraine, for example, a porridge called *kutya*, made from grain and sweetened with honey, is followed by dumplings, fish, cabbage rolls, beans and various vegetables.

Many Guatemalan families enjoy a Christmas tradition of making tamales. A dough called masa, made from corn flour and lard, is spooned onto banana leaves or corn husks before adding a filling of vegetables, pork or chicken, and a tasty sauce. The leaves or husks are folded around the tamales and tied with string and then steamed over boiling water. The outer wrappers are thrown away before the tamales are eaten.

Breads, cakes and sweets of all kinds are also essential Christmas fare around the world. Sometimes the baking work is shared among families or church and community groups. Braided breads are common, often in the shape of a wreath or circle. Special cakes and pies often include the baby Jesus or another Christmas symbol shaped out

Some braided Christmas breads are so fancy, they could double as decorations!
stocknshare/iStock.com

Christmas Unwrapped

Ornaments from around the World

Each year I look forward to decorating a big Christmas tree, not only for the lights, sparkle and cheer it brings to our living room, but also for the chance to unpack my travel ornament collection. About five years ago, my husband and I began to collect ornaments from every city and country we visited. Now, when I take them out of their protective tissue paper, I remember sailing trips to deserted islands, tours of chocolate factories, visits to small Icelandic villages and so much more. In some countries, where Christmas isn't as widely celebrated, I've had to be creative about what an ornament might be. Many magnets and small decorative plates hang from our tree each year, as does a small glass locket containing handmade lace from the tiny Caribbean island of Saba. (DTS)

In the 1930s, Coca-Cola began to run ads with illustrations by artist Haddon Sundblom, who based his image of Santa Claus on a retired traveling salesman he happened to know. These images have strongly influenced how North Americans imagine and depict Santa Claus.

A familiar face decorates this Coca-Cola truck in Manchester, England.
georgeclerk/iStock.com

of dough. In several European countries, as Twelfth Night faded in importance, the Twelfth Night cake became Christmas cake—often with a coin, bean or other little token baked into it. Whoever gets the slice with the coin will have good luck in the coming year.

In the Philippines, *puto bumbong* is a popular dish on Christmas Eve. Sticky purple rice is wrapped and steamed in bamboo tubes before being served with butter, sugar and coconut—a striking addition to any Nochebuena (Christmas Eve) feast table.

Gifts (or Who Brought Those Presents, Anyway?)

Santa Claus as we know him in North America today has been popular since the early twentieth century.

His image was sealed in the 1930s, when Coca-Cola began to use illustrations of him in its Christmas advertising.

Late in World War II, soldiers often dressed up as the North American Santa Claus to bring food and gifts to children in war-torn countries in Western Europe and Asia. This is at least part of the reason why Santa Claus has become popular in so many countries—so popular, in fact, that in some areas the traditional gift-giving characters (such as Saint Nicholas) were nearly erased in favor of Santa Claus. Some countries are working to bring back their traditional gift bringers, while others have brought their own unique twists to the jolly man in red.

In Australia and other countries in the southern hemisphere, Santa arrives during the summer. Given that in Australia temperatures at Christmas can hit over

Some people say that Santa keeps two lists of children's names—one for naughty girls and boys, and one for nice children.
lisegagne/iStock.com

Christmas Unwrapped

Nikki's Christmas on the Beach

Sometimes Christmas traditions do not travel well. When my parents moved from England to Australia in 1963, they took along some very specific ideas about what should be served at Christmas dinner. What my mother hadn't thought about was the fact that in Australia Christmas falls in the middle of summer.

We had no air conditioning, so when the temperature hit 40 degrees Celsius (104 degrees Fahrenheit) in the shade, it was not exactly the best time to cook a turkey. Nevertheless, Mom pushed on. When the bird was finally cooked, it was so hot that none of us could stand the idea of eating a big, hot, heavy meal. It was well after midnight before we were able to eat a bit. (NT)

Even though most of our family lives in Canada, sometimes we travel to a warmer climate to spend Christmas together. Here, we're enjoying the beach in California on Christmas Day.
Nikki Tate

thirty degrees Celsius (eighty-six degrees Fahrenheit), it would hardly be fair for Santa to continue wearing his thick red suit and heavy boots. Santa often changes into shorts and has even been known to do some surfing! A Christmas stamp issued in 1977 shows Santa surfing to shore in his shorts and red jacket. At the time, many people believed that the stamp wasn't serious (or religious) enough for Christmas, but by the time it was re-released in 2007, far fewer people were worried about jolly St. Nick hanging ten.

While many countries share a common tradition in St. Nicholas or Santa bringing gifts and spreading good cheer, he is not the only gift giver found around the world. In Italy, for example, an old lady named ***La Befana*** delivers presents on December 6. Legend has it that the Magi asked her to join them on their journey to Bethlehem, but she wanted to put her house in order first, and she missed out.

She has wandered the skies ever since, looking for the baby Jesus. Like St. Nick, she fills shoes with candy and presents if children have been good, and a lump of coal or a bag of ashes if they have been naughty. Instead of riding on a sleigh pulled by reindeer, she flies through the sky on a broomstick, wrapped in a black shawl. A similar gift bringer in Russia is called the *Baboushka*.

The generally kind witch Befana is not to be confused with the Indo-Germanic witchlike character known as Frau Perchta, who, according to legend, not only gives out rewards during the Twelve Days of Christmas, but also punishes children who have been bad over the past year. According to some stories about her, instead of leaving some coal behind rather than a present, she rips out a person's internal organs and replaces them with straw and pebbles!

La Befana has both candy and coal in her bag of gifts.
Ilyalisse/iStock.com

In Caracas, the capital of Venezuela, the streets are closed to car traffic on Christmas Day so that people can roller-skate to early-morning Mass!

Another scary fellow, *Le Père Fouettard* (Father Whipper, or Father Switch), has been appearing in some regions of France and Belgium from as far back as 1150. Père Fouettard has a scraggly beard, dresses in dark clothes and carries a switch or whip. He travels with Saint Nicholas, or Père Noël, and hands out coal and other punishments to naughty children.

To this day, Icelandic children have to contend with thirteen trolls called the **Yule Lads** and their monstrous house cat, the *Jólakötturinn*, or **Yule Cat**. The trolls used to play nasty tricks on people, but in recent years they've become nicer, leaving toys and sweets in the shoes that children leave in their bedroom window for thirteen days around Christmas. Each of the trolls visits on one of the thirteen nights and leaves small gifts—unless the child

Ded Moroz in front of the Gatchina Palace in Gatchina, Russia.
Oktober64/iStock.com

was naughty the day before, in which case the troll might leave a rotting potato!

Their mythical feline, however, is said to prey on those who don't have new clothes to wear on Christmas Eve. Because people used to be given clothing as a reward for finishing a certain amount of work, the Yule Cat was used as a threat to encourage people to work hard and children to do their chores. If you finished your work and got your new clothes, then the Yule Cat would leave you alone, but if you didn't, you would be at risk of being eaten. Not a very nice Christmas surprise at all! The cat is described in a song called "Jólakötturinn" by the famous Icelandic singer Bjork:

> *His hair sharp as needles*
> *his back was high and bulgy*
> *and claws on his hairy paw*
> *were not a pretty sight...*

Another gift giver is the Eastern European **Ded Moroz** (Grandfather Frost). Like Santa, he is shown wearing fancy velvet robes and delivering presents to children, but he travels via a Russian horse-drawn sleigh known as a *troika*. Ded Moroz first appeared in Russian cities in the mid-1800s. By 1917, the year of the Bolshevik Revolution, Ded Moroz was well established and associated with Christmas. In the 1920s the Bolsheviks tried to get rid of Ded Moroz entirely at the same time as they banned religion and festivals associated with it. In 1935, the Russian leader Joseph Stalin created several nonreligious holidays, including New Year's Day. Ded Moroz and the fir tree were both soon accepted as symbols of the new holiday. Traveling with a star atop his staff, Ded Moroz generally delivers gifts on New Year's Eve or at other parties that take

Christmas Unwrapped

Off with a Bang!

There are Christmas crackers at each place setting at our Christmas dinner table. Shaped like oversized wrapped candies, Christmas crackers are cardboard tubes filled with little toys and sometimes candy, decorated with fancy paper on the outside. They often contain slips of paper with jokes or riddles printed on them, and paper hats shaped like crowns. "Cracker" in the name comes from the strip of paper that runs through the entire tube. Covered with a chemical called silver fulminate, it makes a loud popping noise when broken (or cracked) in half.

Tom Smith of London invented crackers in 1847 as a promotional trick to sell more candy at Christmas.

While evergreen trees are a popular choice in Europe and North America, in India people celebrating Christmas are much more likely to use a mango or banana tree, since few of the fir and spruce trees so common in northern countries grow in hot climates.

Mari Lwyd outside the Bridge Inn in Chepstow, Monmouthshire, Wales.
Andy Dingley/Wikipedia

place leading up to the holiday. He is often shown traveling with Snegurochka, the Snow Maiden, who is believed by some to be his granddaughter.

Fun and Games

Games have been a feature of midwinter celebrations for millennia. Try as it might, the church was never able to stop people from making merry, whether through gambling, dressing up or generally having fun and making mischief. In some countries, these activities remain very much a part of the Christmas festivities. While parlor games such as charades and board games are the norm in some places, things are a little more active in others.

In Ethiopia, for example, boys and men celebrating **Genna** (or **Ganna**), as Christmas is known, play a game with the same name that involves sticks and balls and is a little bit like field hockey. A couple of weeks later, as the country celebrates the baptism of Jesus in a related festival (Timkat), men and boys play another game. **Yeferas guks** is a little bit like jousting mixed with polo. The players wear impressive headdresses made from the manes of lions and adorn their horses with brightly colored decorations on the saddles and bridles. The men on the offensive team use sharp wooden sticks to try to push their opponents off their horses. The defensive team uses only shields (and their reflexes) to protect themselves. In the past, they didn't even use shields, so survival depended totally on skill.

The Ethiopians aren't the only ones to celebrate Christmas with an equine (horse) activity. An old Welsh Christmas tradition, revived in recent years, called **Mari Lwyd**, involves groups of men going from door to door in their village, singing and asking for food and drink. The group takes along a pretend horse, often made of a horse skull fastened to a pole. A sheet draped behind the skull falls over the shoulders of the man carrying the pole, hiding him from view. A horse handler pretends to try to keep the horse under control as the revelers move through the streets. When the group approaches a house and calls out a request to enter and be given a snack and a drink, the residents call back, and then a noisy but playful debate follows about whether the horse and his troupe should be allowed in.

SUGAR COOKIES

Have fun decorating these simple sugar cookies before Christmas, and then set out a couple to energize Santa as he travels around the world. Don't forget to leave a carrot for Rudolph and his friends!

Ingredients:

1 cup butter
1 cup white sugar
1 egg
1 teaspoon vanilla
2 cups all-purpose flour
1 teaspoon salt
Icing or sprinkles as desired

Directions:

Preheat oven to 350 degrees F. Lightly grease some cookie sheets. In a bowl, cream butter and sugar together. Add egg and vanilla, and beat well. Add flour and salt, and mix until a soft dough forms. Chill dough in the fridge for 1 hour. On a floured board, roll the dough out to a thickness of about ⅛ inch. Use seasonal cookie cutters to cut dough into shapes, and transfer them to cookie sheets. Bake for 4 to 6 minutes or until the bottoms of the cookies are lightly browned. If you ended up with thicker cookies, you will need to bake for slightly longer. Cool cookies before decorating them as desired.

Dani's German Christmases

This was my favorite gift the year I turned five. One of the benefits of living in Florida was being able to ride my bike right away!
Nikki Tate

Although my family has German roots, by the time I was born in the late 1980s, my *oma* (grandmother) had been living outside Germany for over twenty years, and we did not follow many day-to-day German traditions. Beyond a deep love of cervelat (a type of salami popular in Germany, Switzerland and France) and liverwurst, shared by my entire family, 364 days of the year I have never felt particularly German.

That all changes when we celebrate Christmas in the family's German tradition, opening our Christmas gifts and having our main celebration on Christmas Eve. As far as I was (and still am) concerned when I was growing up, there were several benefits to this system. I loved not having to wait for yet another night before Santa arrived, and it was the one night of the year when I could stay up as late as I wanted to. I much preferred that to waking up early! I have always loved the entire day of anticipation and last-minute preparations leading up to the fall of darkness on Christmas Eve, and the coziness of the evening spent with family, eating, celebrating and sharing gifts.

The year I turned five, we lived near Miami, Florida, and our house didn't have a chimney. How was Santa supposed to get into the house? My mom created her own tradition, which served several purposes. At about three o'clock in the afternoon I went to have a nap, and since I had trouble falling sleep because I was so excited, she would read me "The Night before Christmas." She explained that Santa visited the German households first and then doubled back around for everyone else. (Those poor, tired reindeer!) This meant he arrived at our house right around dusk, waking me from my nap with the ringing of his bells and stomping of his feet. After I raced out of my room, I discovered that he had entered the house through the sliding glass doors, eaten his snack and left some goodies behind.

When my uncle married his British wife and they had children, they couldn't decide which tradition to keep. Instead of picking one or the other, they reached a compromise—all gifts exchanged between family members are opened on Christmas Eve. On Christmas morning, each child opens another special present delivered by Santa during the night. Gifts from Santa are wrapped with paper that is different from any other presents under the tree.

My oma loved Christmas and was eager to share her traditions with me, including an annual visit to Santa.
Nikki Tate

Renata's Story

Renata dressed up to visit Santa and was given a small gift—paid for by her parents but handed out by Santa—before leaving.

Valz Family

Renata Valz grew up in Georgetown, Guyana, a former British colony in South America. With its diverse mix of Caribbean, African, Portuguese, Amerindian, East Indian, Chinese and British cultures, Guyana enjoys many unique traditions and events.

"Christmas was one of the most exciting days of the year," Renata remembers, adding that only Easter was more exciting. "Christmas truly brings everyone together in celebration," she says, though coming together is less about the religious aspects of the season, perhaps because the population is made up of Christians, Hindus, Muslims and people who practice other religions.

In Guyana the celebration has become a "melting pot" of cultural traditions. One of the most common dishes to eat on Christmas morning is pepper pot, a traditional Amerindian dish featuring stewed meat, spices and a sauce made from the cassava root. Renata says you'd be disappointed if you went to someone's house around Christmas and weren't offered some. Popular drinks of the season include mauby (made from the bark of the mauby tree), sorrel and ginger beer.

Another key menu item is black cake—or rum cake—a fruit cake containing alcohol and a special type of caramelized brown sugar that makes it look black. Women soak the fruit in alcohol for up to six months before Christmas, which makes this a very strongly flavored dessert! Cloves, fruit, wine and the rum Guyana is famous for may all make their way into black cake.

Foods such as grapes and apples are also often imported for Christmas. "Since they were a once-a-year treat," Renata says, "[these fruits] were one of the most exciting aspects of Christmas."

Renata remembers her parents taking her to see Santa Claus. Looking back, she finds the exerience interesting because someone from any cultural group could be wearing Santa clothes, not just an older white man who has a beard.

There are no chimneys in Guyana, so Renata's father told her that Santa entered the house through the keyhole. Some families leave the door unlocked or leave a key out for Santa.

"Every year at Christmas, we did our version of spring cleaning," Renata recalls. Women might also get large seasonal floral arrangements to decorate their houses. Typically, these weren't live flowers but a faux-flower arrangement in a vase large enough to sit on your floor."

Because many people leave Guyana to get work or an education, to live with family or to seek out a better life abroad, family members may be far-flung. Renata remembers her favorite Christmas, the year she was ten: "The best part of that wasn't just getting a piano, but having the whole family together. It was one of the first Christmases where all of the family members from my dad's side were in Guyana. My cousins, my dad's sisters—everyone was there. Just being able to spend time with family members that you rarely saw made it really special."

Pepper pot is a popular dish in Guyana at Christmas.
Wikipedia

Some Russian nesting dolls (matryoshka) are decorated with Christmas themes.
Dmitry Fisher/iStock.com

A final word from the authors

Whether we choose to celebrate a more religious or a more secular version of the holiday, Christmas is rooted in universal themes we can all agree on—family, friendship, love and light. We hope you enjoyed reading this book and that you too had some aha moments about why your family does some of the things you've taken for granted year after year. Perhaps you've even become inspired to start a new tradition in your family—how will you make it your very own? We are going to bring back the tradition of making paper chains to help decorate the house. All the grandchildren can take part in a big garland-making party! We are also excited about trying some of the new foods we discovered when working on this book, particularly the Guyanese pepper pot—though we might save that for lunch or dinner and stick to cinnamon buns for Christmas breakfast!

A note from the series editor

"The Origins are built on the bedrock of personal stories, enhanced by careful research and illuminated by stunning photographs. No book can be all things to all people, and no two people experience a culture in the same way. The Origins are not meant to be the definitive word on any culture or belief; instead they will lead readers toward a place where differences are acknowledged and knowledge facilitates understanding."

—Sarah N. Harvey

Fifth Avenue illuminated at night in Playa del Carmen, Mexico.
anouchka/iStock.com

GLOSSARY

Advent—the first season of the Christian church year, beginning on the fourth Sunday before Christmas and lasting until Christmas Eve.

Advent calendar—a calendar used to count the days leading up to Christmas. A flap opened each day reveals a seasonal image or small gift.

Baboushka—a traditional gift-giving figure in Russia.

BCE—before the Common Era, referring to the years before the start of year one in the current calendar. See CE.

carol—a religious song expressing joy, most often associated with Christmas.

CE—Common Era. A nonreligious method of numbering the years beginning after what was traditionally believed to be the birth date of Jesus Christ.

Christianity—a major world religion focused on the life and teachings of Jesus Christ.

Ded Moroz (Old Man Frost or Grandfather Frost)—a Russian gift-giving character similar to Santa Claus.

Epiphany—a Christian feast day, in most years falling on January 6, that celebrates the revelation of Jesus Christ's divinity and usually focuses on the arrival of the Magi to see the baby Jesus, and Jesus's later baptism in the Jordan River.

frankincense—a fragrant essential oil used in perfumes and incense.

Genna (or Ganna)—the Ethiopian name for Christmas, celebrated on January 7.

globos—colorful paper lanterns with small candles inside them.

La Befana—a traditional gift-giving figure in Italy.

Le Père Fouettard (Father Whipper or Father Switch)—in the folklore of some parts of France and Belgium, a character who travels with Saint Nicholas and hands out presents to good children and sticks or lumps of coal to children who have been naughty.

Magi—biblical figures, also known as the three wise men or the three kings, said to have brought presents to the newly born baby Jesus.

Mari Lwyd—a folk tradition from Wales in which singing men take a pretend horse from house to house, hoping to receive food and drink.

Middle Ages—the period of time in European history lasting from approximately the fifth century through the fifteenth.

myrrh—a resin extracted from a type of thorny bush or tree and used to make perfume, incense and medicine.

Nativity—in the Christian tradition, the birth of Jesus.

New Testament—the second part of the Christian Bible, describing the life and teachings of Jesus and his followers.

northern hemisphere—the half of the earth lying north of the equator.

Puritans—a group of Christians in the fifteenth and sixteenth centuries who wanted to simplify and purify church practices.

Saint Nicholas—a Turkish bishop from the fourth century who became known as the patron saint of children and sailors.

Saturnalia—an ancient Roman festival honoring the god Saturn.

solstice—the shortest (winter) and longest (summer) day of each year.

southern hemisphere—the half of the earth lying south of the equator.

Twelfth Night—the last night of the Christmas season in the Christian tradition.

Twelve Days of Christmas—the time between Christmas and Epiphany in the Christian tradition.

yeferas guks—an Ethiopian jousting game played on horseback.

Yule Cat—an unpleasant character in Icelandic mythology who punishes people for being naughty.

Yule Lads—thirteen trolls said to leave small gifts for children during the Christmas season in Iceland.

yule log—a large piece of wood burned in the fireplace during the Christmas season.

Christmas market in Hyde Park, London, England.
iStock.com

RESOURCES

Chapter One

Print:

Elliott, Jock. *Inventing Christmas: How Our Holiday Came to Be*. New York: Harry N. Abrams, 2002.

Online:

The History Channel: "History of Christmas."
history.com/topics/christmas/history-of-christmas

The Colonial Williamsburg Foundation: "Christmas in Colonial Virginia."
history.org/Foundation/journal/autumn99/inva.cfm?

Christianity Today: "The Face of Christmas Past."
christianitytoday.com/history/2009/december/face-of-christmas-past.html

Biography: "St. Nicholas."
biography.com/people/st-nicholas-204635

Chapter Two

Print:

Allen, Linda. *Decking the Halls: The Folklore and Traditions of Christmas Plants*.
Minocqua, WI: Willow Creek Press, 2000.

Bowler, Gerry. *Santa Claus: A Biography*. Toronto, ON: McClelland & Stewart, 2007.

Greenwood, Barbara and Heather Collins (illustrator). *A Pioneer Christmas: Celebrating in the Backwoods in 1841*. Toronto, ON: Kids Can Press, 2003.

Online:

BBC Berkshire: "Queen Victoria popularised our Christmas traditions."
news.bbc.co.uk/local/berkshire/hi/people_and_places/history/newsid_9286000/9286971.stm

The Hymns and Carols of Christmas.
hymnsandcarolsofchristmas.com

Wikipedia: "James Lord Pierpont."
en.m.wikipedia.org/wiki/James_Lord_Pierpont

Chapter Three

Print:

Bowler, Gerry. *The World Encyclopedia of Christmas*. Toronto, ON: McClelland & Stewart, 2004.

Holder, Judith and Alison Harding. *Christmas Fare*. Devon, UK: Webb and Bower Limited, 1981.

Mandryk, DeeAnn. *Canadian Christmas Traditions: Festive Recipes and Stories from Coast to Coast*. Calgary, AB: Altitude Publishing, 2005.

Online:

National Geographic: "St. Nicholas to Santa: The Surprising Origins of Mr. Claus."
news.nationalgeographic.com/news/2013/12/131219-santa-claus-origin-history-christmas-facts
-st-nicholas/?rptregcta=reg_free_np&rptregcampaign=20131016_rw_membership_r1p_us_dr_w

Whychristmas?com: "Christmas Fun, Games & Activities."
whychristmas.com/fun/

INDEX

*Page numbers in **bold** indicate an image; there may also be text related to the same topic on that page*

Acknowledgments

My life would not be as wonderful as it is without my amazing family. And this book would not have been possible without several generations' worth of Christmas passion! Each year, despite crazy work and travel schedules, somehow we manage to come together to celebrate and spend time together. Dani is doing an exceptional job of heading up the next generation of seasonal devotees and was the one who thought we should do this book. I can't think of anyone who could have brought more enthusiasm to the project than she has. The team at Orca Book Publishers continues to be an outstanding example of a dream publishing house. The book looks beautiful thanks to Rachel Page, makes sense thanks to Sarah Harvey's firm editorial hand and will find an audience thanks to a whole slew of people who work tirelessly to make sure Orca books make their way into the hands of readers around the world. Merrie-Ellen Wilcox pushed us to dig deeper and question everything. Various academics, including Oscar Swan, Timothy Tangherlini, Mary Beard, Jeanmarie Rouhier-Willoughby and Richard Seaford, patiently answered our questions and provided guidance in their respective areas of expertise. Any misinterpretations, omissions or errors are ours alone.

—NT

As always, many thanks to my co-author and mom, Nikki—at this point I can't imagine doing one of these books on my own, so you are stuck with me now! Thanks especially for letting me indulge my passion for all things Christmas with this book! Toryn, thank you for everything, not least of which is counting the days to Christmas every year, always starting on December 26. You certainly know how to put a smile on my face! And, of course, a huge thank-you to everyone at Orca! I'm so lucky to be supported by such an amazing Canadian publishing house. Sarah Harvey's gentle but always spot-on guidance toward clarity and coherence is extremely appreciated (especially after the rewrites are complete!), and I am so in love with Rachel Page's design and ever grateful for her patience as I hunt down family photos. To the many others behind the scenes, thank you so much for all you do to support Canadian publishing. I know my thanks are echoed by many.

—DTS

Explore Diversity

with the Orca Origins

Award-winning authors dig deep into the cultures that shaped them as they connect with and explain **traditions that have nourished and supported people for centuries**. Filled with rich personal stories, carefully researched history, gorgeous photos (and some delicious recipes), the Orca Origins provide vital connections to **the magnificent diversity of our modern world**.

9781459809901 • 24.95 HC

"A must-have title."
—Jewish Book Council

9781459810075 • 24.95 HC

"An exceptionally valuable resource."
—Kirkus Reviews

9781459812970 • 24.95 HC

"Capture[s] the essence of what makes these celebrations special and piques the interest of the reader."
—School Library Connection

9781459811263 • 24.95 HC

"Uniquely personal stories make this book stand out...Kids who think they know about this holiday will be surprised at the new things they learn."
—Booklist

9781459811812 • 24.95 HC

"A good choice for learning about Muslims' traditions as expressed in various cultures."
—Kirkus Reviews

Forthcoming

9781459812234 • 24.95 HC

Powwow
Karen Pheasant-Naganigwane

NONFICTION FOR AGES 9-12

ORCA BOOK PUBLISHERS
orcabook.com • 1-800-210-5277

Orca Origins

orcaorigins.com